Lurid and Insane
Comfort Hour
Marginal Notes
Come Together

a musical, an hour of radio,
a monologue and a play
by Stan's Cafe

ISBN 978-1-913185-19-0

Published by Stan's Cafe
Birmingham, UK
2020

www.stanscafe.co.uk

Lurid and Insane © Stan's Cafe 2001
Photos © Ed Dimsdale 2001
Comfort Hour © Stan's Cafe 2008
Photo © Ed Dimsdale 2008
Marginal Notes © Stan's Cafe 1999
Photo © Graeme Rose 1994
Come Together © Stan's Cafe 2008
Photo © Alicia Rogalska
Publication © Stan's Cafe 2020

Contents:

Lurid and Insane   1

Bonus Material
Credits   26
Comfort Hour   27
Raw text for *Comfort Hour*   28
Performing *Lurid and Insane*   29
Marginal Notes   34
Come Together   36

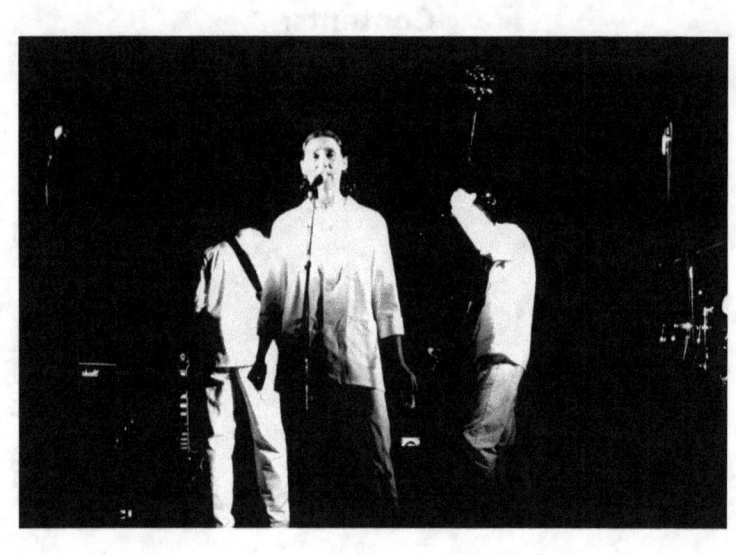

Lurid and Insane

Overture
[The band arrive on stage one at a time. They start playing as they arrive, building excitement, anticipating the president's arrival],

Amanda: Good evening everyone. I'm sorry about the slight delay in proceedings. You'll appreciate that the President has a very busy schedule at the moment, but we've been told that he has left his meeting in Leeds and is in the air now. Thank you for bearing with us.

It's fantastic to see you all here. This is a very exciting night for the party and a particularly special night for some of us here in the band, as of course this is home ground. I'm overwhelmed to see so many familiar faces. We think of Edinburgh *[substitute venue's location]* as the place where it all started. I know the President feels the same. Tonight we hope to show you our thanks.

I've just been told that the President's helicopter is over the city now. He should be landing within the next few minutes. This just gives me time to make a few announcements.

Security have been handed a blue rucksack, if anyone has lost a blue rucksack please contact security or a member of the crew. I must remind you that any unattended bags will be confiscated.

Security have also asked us to close the bar during the event.

We've asked for no press photographs during the event. There will be an official press conference announced later this week, but tonight is for the people. Any unauthorised members of the press found with cameras or recording equipment will be escorted from the venue.

[Sounds of a helicopter landing close by]

Can I also take this opportunity to lay to rest the rumours that have been circulating over the last two weeks about the president's health... well it seems that you'll be able to see for yourselves.

[The President's microphone is added to its stand by a roadie]

The President has landed and is on his way to the venue now. Please stand away from the doors at the back of the hall.

Welcome

[The President walks through the auditorium, shaking audience members by the hand. Arriving on stage, he greets the band before addressing the crowd – this speech is rewritten to make it specific for each venue]

President: Now is a whirly-gig mercury time.
A joyful time of history waiting.
This moment is the culmination of a thousand moments.
We are paused on the edge of all that is beautiful.

– music –

Flying in over Edinburgh, wheeling in through clouds and turbulence until, at a thousand feet, everything comes clear and still; a jewellery box scattered in the rocks shining through phosphorescent heather, a sash of golden sunlit Firth, a City in celebration.

We land in Princes' Park and as the motorcade sweeps through these grand roads, I gasp at the energy and joy of the revellers in victory.
I'm humbled to be here. Be proud of what you have done here.

I am pleased to welcome you
I can feel your love
I can feel your power
Welcome to the party

Band: Welcome *[chorus]*

President: I welcome the familiar faces and our loyal friends from Yorkshire and London.
You have made the journey and continue to make the journey.
The Birmingham Posse, some of the original crew,

you were there for us, now we're here for you.
And the Party's international section, it took us a long time to win through,
but we're there now.
We're everywhere. Everywhere!

Band: Welcome [chorus]

President: This party was built from one mind, then it was two, then hundreds, now thousands, everyone sharing the vision.
Some minds were clouded, shrouded in a fog of dizzy thinking, now they all shine diamond clear, bright and hard.
It's not my Party or your Party or their Party but our Party.
The party has grown with us and of us.
New members, this is your Party as well.
This is everyone's Party and everyone is welcome
Let's sing it... lets sing it!
Come on! Come on!

Band: Welcome [chorus]

Party Song

President: Some of you may know this one, join in if you can.

– music –

We've been waiting too long to party
Now we're here it's gonna last forever
We've been waiting too long to party
Now we're here it's gonna last forever

Make way for the movers
Stand back for the swingers
Hold on to your Party Card girl
Hands up if we're feelin' fine
Jump up or you're stood up
Make time for a good time

Hold on to your Party Card boy
Hands up and prepare to dance coz...

It's time to celebrate!

We've been waiting too long to party
Now we're here it's gonna last forever *[etc.]*

Switched on by the music
Pumped up by the bass drum
Hold on to your Party Card girl
Hands up if you hear this sound
Tune out bad vibrations
Pug this whole new sound
Hold onto your Party Card boy
Hands up and hold your breath coz...

It's time to celebrate!

We've been waiting too long to party
Now we're here it's gonna last forever *[etc.]*

Manifesto

President: You know, people often say to me, "the world's a complicated place, how do you make sense of it all?" In answer to these people I say, "the world's not complicated, it's just big and being big doesn't make it difficult to make sense of".

I used to think the world was complicated but, once I'd started to study it carefully, I began to find simple patterns emerging. These patterns were repeated everywhere I looked in every aspect of life. I soon realised that to understand the world all you need to do is understand its pattern. In the face of the pattern all knots unravel themselves. It's simple.

	Most of you will know this one, join in where you can. Craig, let's teach them the pattern.
Craig:	Here set out, are the three books of state.

Book 1: Love

Craig:	How do we spell love?
Band:	L.O.V.E.
Craig:	True: any other spelling refers to a degraded form of the notion. The term love should not be used in any demeaning context; such as in combination with the words: 'up', 'free', 'monster' or 'puppy'. Love should not be commodified or quantified; love should therefore not be referred to as 'it'. Love has no meaning if it is not expressed in actions.
Amanda:	Act on love.
President:	Let's love!
Craig:	Take care and be taken care of.
Amanda:	Protect and be protected.
Graeme	War is defence, defence is love, love is war.
Craig:	Individuals shall not be able to go to war, such an act would be deemed an act of unilateral love and as such not love but a perversion of the love concept.
Amanda:	The perversion of love is a great crime.
Craig:	Ill concern, casual harm and all other anti-love acts are criminal and should be punished.
Amanda:	Question:
Craig:	How may crime be punished if the act of punishment is itself deemed harmful?
Amanda:	Answer:
Craig:	The short term harm caused by injurious punishment fades to leave the lasting rectitude of good, correct behaviour.
Amanda:	Question:
Craig:	What's the cost of failing to penalise crime?
Amanda:	Answer:
Craig:	Further crime.

Amanda:	Punishing crime eradicates future crime
Craig:	This is an act of...
Band:	Love!
Amanda:	Question:
Craig:	If the love of the improved individual is added to the love of the crime prevented what does punishment equal?
Band:	Love love.
C&A:	Double Love.
President:	We double love for you by beating those that harm you.

Let's Groove!

Book 2: Groove

Craig:	Question:
Amanda:	What's Groove?
Craig:	Answer:
Amanda:	Whilst love circumscribes our relations to each other, the Groove represents our relationship to ourselves.
Craig:	Groove represents flexibility of thinking the power and freedom to choose between A and B, the chance to live in, respond to and anticipate 'the movement'.
President:	Let's move!
Craig:	The Groove notes that we are all bound together, as one nation, moving as one. It also confirms that, within this one movement we each have our own styles, our own tempos. The Groove is undeniable and universal, easy to follow, difficult to instigate.
Amanda:	It requires that some are disciplined so others can be loose.
Craig:	Some must be tight so that others can let go.
President:	Let go!

President:	Question:
Craig:	In the war between socialism and market economics what is the only theory and belief system that circles the squares and lets loose the juice of pleasure over penury?
Band:	Groove!
Craig:	In the Groove no one gets hurt, everyone wins.
President:	Relaxation is crucial. Disengage with your brain, think with your feet and make these shapes.
Nina:	Choose your clothes carefully, they show you and your peers off in the best light. Don't mix blue and black. Don't wear dark tops with light trousers, skirts over leggings. Beige is the colour of compromise and thus should be avoided.
Band:	Groove
Craig:	is what raises us above other nations.
Band:	Groove
Craig:	is the right to be different and treated the same.
Band:	Groove!
Amanda:	Grooving is everybody's duty.
Craig:	Everyone loves better when they are relaxed.
Amanda:	Everyone works better if they are happy.
Craig:	The Groove is therefore central to life and the state.
Amanda:	To fail to Groove at the appointed time is a crime.
Craig:	The Groove and good times are only possible when everyone is joining in.
C&A:	So join in! Groove!
N&G:	There is no fascism that is groovy. There is no fascism that is groovy. Groovy is alternative thinking. Groovy is alternative thinking. Fascism does not allow for alternative thinking.

	Fascism does not allow for alternative thinking. There is no alternative to Groove that is not un-groovy.
	There is no alternative to Groove that is not un-groovy.
C&A:	Fight for your party and its right to Groove, Groove!
President:	LET'S WORK! *[The president takes the band through their solos he gets the Work Dance going and leads a call and response]* WORK LOVE GROOVE!

[Song ends]

Testify

Amanda: Three years ago I was a lonely person. If you'd told me I was lonely I would have laughed at you, but I was. I went out with people from work after work, but when they went home I stayed, I stayed and drank. And before too long I began to think I had only one true friend, this *[Holds up bottle]*. I was lonely and unhappy and if I'd been sober enough to see it, I'd have recognised that I was losing all I had fought for over the years. I was having trouble holding my job down. I had only one true loyalty, to this. I was in a spiral of decline there was only one constant in my life, this. I clang to this as if it were a life-raft, not recognising that it was this that was dragging me under.

Then, one day I was in a bar, inevitably. It was early, the place was quiet, the door opened from the street and out of the summer light stepped a figure, a man. And, at a time when no one spoke to me and everyone avoided me and everyone judged me, this man walked in and he didn't judge me, he didn't moralise or ignore me; he just walked up to me, bought me a drink and asked me my name. Before I knew it I was telling him the story of my life. He never once blinked or looked away; he listened, really listened and it was as if, by getting me to speak it, he was draining all the badness, all the poisons out of me. That night, for the first time in months, I walked home sober and slept with a peace of mind that came not from this, but from knowing I could take control of my own life.

He, this man, he walked into my life. He said things, things that made such sense to me, things I'd been wanting to hear. He touched me, deeply, like I'd never been touched before and that was it for me, from then on, that was all I needed. I've not touched a drop since. I've pulled my life out of it's nose dive. I won't say I wasn't ever tempted, I was, but on those occasions all I had to do was seek this man out and he would put it right for me again. He always had time for me, he still does, despite everything. I count him as a friend and tonight I want to say thank you to my friend.

Graeme: Amazing, you know sometimes I look down and I can't believe my own eyes. You know less than twelve months ago I wouldn't have dared step on this. I wouldn't have had the confidence to stand on this stage and talk to you like this. That's because, less than twelve months ago I was a big man, I weighed twenty three stone. I was overweight, I was. I'd let myself go.

Then one day I was beside the road, in North Wales, it was the A525 just east of Mold (some of you may know it) I was hitchhiking, no one had passed for hours, it was a Sunday. It had been raining, dusk was approaching and dark clouds were gathering again when a white Mercedes swept over the crest of the hill and swung down towards me. I never believed for a moment that a car like that would stop, but it did and little did I know, as I squeezed myself onto the back seat, amidst all those leaflets and posters, that my life was about to change.

Who was the driver that gloomy Autumn evening? Whose eyes met mine in the rear view mirror that day? Those were the eyes of the man who would drive me down the long and sometimes twisting road that has led to me being here tonight. I've never felt happier, I've never felt fitter. I didn't think I had it in me. I'm eleven stone two and so proud to be able to stand here in front of you all and thank this man for stopping for me that day. I will always be loyal to this man.

Now I want to give him some thing back I want to TESTIFY!

Band: Testify [chorus]

Simon: Tonight, I want to issue you a challenge and I hope you are going to respond to it. We all feel secure living within the envelope of what we know we can achieve, The Comfort Zone we call it. I've lived my life by setting my self challenges and achieving them.

At 18 I set myself the challenge to become a millionaire, by twenty three I'd done it. I had houses on three continents, a fleet of cars, motorbikes. I threw week long parties. All my girlfriends were models.

I didn't know it but I was coasting. Then, at the biggest party I'd every thrown, I met this man. "I'm putting a band together" he said "I don't want your money, I want you to play the drums". This seemed ludicrous. At first I thought I couldn't afford to do it, then I began to think maybe I couldn't afford not to do it. That day I gave this man my fortune and the keys to my yacht, I took up the sticks and never returned to work. I've closed some big deals in my time but I'm strongly convinced this is the biggest and best decision I will ever take. We don't get paid much to be in this band, we do it because we love it and believe in it and I'd do it for free. I don't need my wages, I don't need this *[Takes wallet out of pocket]*, I'm going to give him this too.

I challenge you to listen to the stories that you hear tonight. Listen to what this man says and ask yourselves: can I afford not to take up the challenge?

Craig:	Now tell us Nina, what's your story?
Nina:	It's not very special.
Craig:	Everyone's story's special Nina, tell us why you're here.
Nina:	I got chosen.
Craig:	Chosen to be in the band? Really, who by?
Nina:	I got chosen by my friends from home.
Craig:	They said you should come to the audition?
Nina:	Yes.
Craig:	And then your playing just spoke for itself I presume.
Nina:	No, my hair got me in.
Craig:	It's great hair, just the kind of hair a guitarist needs.
Nina:	That's what my friends said.
Craig:	So how long have you been playing now?
Nina:	Three weeks.
Craig:	Three weeks!
Nina:	I've been learning fast.
Craig:	That's amazing, how have you managed?
Nina:	Once you're in a band you can't let anyone down, you have to do what you can. Three weeks ago I was on maracas, now I'm lead guitarist. You have to rise to the challenge.
Craig	You've heard it ladies and gentlemen three weeks

Nina	ago she was on maracas, now lead guitar! Come on everyone, come up here, come up and testify.

Craig:	For some this may be considered an act of madness. *[Opens up umbrella]* For some of you, good rational God fearing people though you may consider yourselves to be, this seems reckless. Opening an umbrella indoors, new shoes on the table, hats resting on beds, a solitary magpie espied on a fence; all bad omens or acts inviting mishap, possibly even tragedy. Some of you may at this moment be crossing your fingers, hoping to ward off whatever disaster I have invited.
	I used to be like that, barely able to live my life for dodging cracks in the pavement, holding my breath, afraid to turn out the light for fear of inviting monsters out from under the bed. But now I don't care, look at me! I know I have power

over my own life. I make decisions for myself, fate has no hold on me. This man showed me that strength and courage, decisiveness and clarity of thought will always win out over superstition and a surrender to fate. Our dreams do not dictate our future. We must be prepared to work courageously to make our dreams our future. This is the most important lesson of my life, it was taught to me by this man, by his words and the actions that backed them up.

I've learnt my lesson and I've followed and trusted in him ever since. I urge you to do the same, uncross your fingers, take control of your lives, come up here and TESTIFY.

Band: Testify *[chorus]*

[Amanda asks if anyone in the audience would like to come up to share their testimony]

Heather: *[From the audience in every day clothes]* Wow! Hello Edinburgh!

I, well I just had this feeling that I had to come up here and meet you all, to meet you. I have this incredible feeling of belonging. Your stories really touched me out there, it felt that you were talking directly to me. I feel understood in a way I've not experienced before. I can't believe this is happening I never do anything like this!

I really hope this is going to change my life and I nearly didn't come here tonight, my mum (I live with my mum), she wasn't too keen that I came here on my own, I was going to come with my boyfriend but we had an argument.

We've not been getting on that well lately, in fact we've been fighting a lot but I was really hoping that we'd sort it out, cos we were saving to move in together. I really shouldn't still be living with my mum, we don't get on that well and there really isn't room for me there anymore, she's already half taken over my bedroom with her sewing machine (she makes quilts for people).

So I've been working in the chippy round the corner to earn a bit of money to move out, its not a great job, in fact its a terrible job, I serve chips all day and smell of the chip fat all the time. I'm sorry if I smell, I did my best to get rid of it, but I don't know what's going to happen now.

I don't think things are going to be the same anymore, I'm so sorry that my boyfriend's not here tonight. I wish I could have convinced him to come. He plays in a band, nothing like this one, he's been doing it for about five years, he plays the guitar but he is no way as good as you. He would have loved this gig!

I don't see how I can go back now, he won't understand, things just aren't going to be the same anymore, I can't believe that he's missing this, its his own fault, I've been talking about coming here all week. I saw your posters in town and knew I had to come tonight and now I know why!

This is the best thing that could have happened to me. I really feel as though this is a turning point for me, that now I can move on, that my life as it is has been changed for ever, I can't believe he's missing this, I wish he was here to share this with me, wow this is amazing, I feel like I can tell you everything that I can get it all out and its okay, that you'll listen and make it better, somehow make it better.

Band: Testify [chorus]

[The President hypnotises the band]

President: Simon, tell me the square root of 13.
Simon: [Starts reciting a very long string of numbers the first few of which at least are the square root of 13 they run under much of what follows]
President: Nina, what is the world's longest river?
Nina: The Amazon.
President: How long is it?
Nina: 1034 miles.
President: How wide is it at it's widest point?
Nina: 150 miles.
President: What's it's cubic volume.
Nina 60,000 gallons per minutes.
President: Craig, you're asleep.

Craig:	*[Sleeps, standing up]*
President:	Claude, you are Martin Luther King.
Graeme:	*[Starts the MLK 'I have a dream' speech which runs under much of what follows]*
President:	Nina, name the chart positions of all of Cliff Richard's hit singles.
Nina:	*[Starts reeling off numbers]*
President:	Simon, tell me the names of the grandparents of all of the members of tonight's audience.
Simon:	*[Switches to reciting names]*
President:	Claude, conduct Beethoven's fifth symphony.
Graeme:	*[Stops MLK and starts silently conducting]*
President:	We have the whole of the world here, all of knowledge is at hand; who wants to ask a question? Anything, ask me anything.
Audience:	How are you going to reduce crime?
President:	Nina, how many crimes are committed in this country each year?
Nina:	Five million, two hundred and thirty four thousand, four hundred and thirty six.
President:	What is the country's population?
Nina:	Fifty eight million, seven hundred and eighty nine thousand, one hundred and ninety four.
President:	So divide one by the other, how many crimes do we each commit per year?
Nina:	0.089
President:	How much do we currently spend on policing and justice?
Nina:	£29 billion
President:	So if we all reduced the crimes we committed by 0.03 how much money would we each save?
Nina:	£327.
President:	Think about it, it's all money in your pocket.
Amanda:	I believe Heather has a question Mr. President.
Heather:	Is there life on other planets?
President:	Life on other planets? I can tell you there is and I've spoken to them. Simon, let's see if we can make contact. I can't guarantee this will work but while Simon

	tunes in, let's find another question.
	[A genuine question is taken from a real audience member]
Amanda:	I can tell what you're really asking is, "am I losing my animal magnetism?"
President:	Thank you for sharing that, it shows a lot of trust *[leads applause]*.
	[To Heather, indicating the questioner]
	Is this an attractive man?
Heather:	Yes.
President:	On a scale of one to ten how attractive?
Heather:	Eight.
President:	What are the five most crucial elements of attractiveness, Nina?
Nina:	Eyes, hands, smile, dress sense, confidence.
President:	In what area does this man score lowest?
Nina:	Confidence.
President:	You are lacking in confidence because you are not following the Work Love Groove ethic. Follow that and your confidence will return.
Simon	*[Alien voice]*
President:	Craig, translate for us.
Craig:	"Good evening everyone, it is great to be able to join you at this special occasion. it is good to see so much hard work come to fruition. The music is sounding good, enjoy the party."
Amanda:	I know this is unusual but does anyone have a question to ask the alien?

[Audience question and alien's response]

Amanda:	Is there an issue, anything that's important in your life. What is our policy on....?

[Audience contribution]

President:	That's a great question. If you give your name and address to Amanda she will send you our policy document on that.
Amanda:	We're all worried about the future.
President:	I'm moved by that.
	I'll tell you what I'm going to do.
	I'm going to share something with you.

[The President is brought an acoustic guitar and a high stool. With the band off stage the president accompanies himself singing a quiet, reflective number]

My Way

President: Guiding Beacon on the darkest night
Desert shade and mountain sign
Warming blanket in the wildest storm
We've been together through it all

I'm often lonely
I'm sometimes tired
but

If you can't walk beside me
Then I'll lead the way
If you can't walk beside me
Then I'll lead the way

Stepping stones across th' angry river
Truest arrow in the shaking quiver
Shining bridge cross the widest call
We've been together through it all

Keenest knife - when the ghosts want purgin
Steadying hand in the smoke a confusion
Safety net to break the fall
We've been together through it all

If you can't walk beside me
Then I'll lead the way
If you can't walk beside me
Then I'll lead the way
But if things don't work out
then we'll do it my way

[By the end of the song the band have returned to give backing vocals. At the emotional climax of the song a shot rings out and the President falls to the floor]

[The President falls and is carried off stage by the band]

Graeme:	Don't panic, stay calm! All the doors have been locked, nobody leave.
Amanda:	*[Returning to the stage]* I'm sorry to say the president has been shot, but he's not dead! Now I'm going to bring the band back on, it's what he would have wanted.
Graeme:	Music is a great healer.
Nina:	As a tribute to the president I'd like to play his favourite strong. *[Plays opening riff from Smoke on the Water then dissolves into tears]*
Graeme:	I've been writing a three part symphony. *[Plays 'prog jazz' bass solo with drum accompaniment]*
Heather:	I too would like to give my tribute to the President. *[She gets the band to join an a cappella rendition of Yesterday, she breaks off singing 'why he had to go']*

Craig: Let's think on him in our hearts and in our brains
Simon: I've got great news! The president's condition has stabilised. Our challenge now is to bring him back. What we need to do is will him back. Let's will him back.

Message from Jonathan
[A series of messages and bizarre gifts are brought through the auditorium and from the wings. This section is largely improvised around the following]
Heather: Text message from Rachel and Steve.
Graeme: A flower from the bar ladies.
Nina: Bill and Gee.
Amanda: E-mails are flooding in.
Craig: People are gathering outside.
Heather: Get well card and bag of plumbs.
Graeme: You will be wanting to make your own tributes.
Simon: Readers digest.
Craig: Frank Bruno.

Graeme: Mantovani.
Amanda: It's often the small gifts...

Heather:	This is from Elton John! *[Gold plated Flymo]*
Simon:	From Moseley Junior School.
Graeme:	The President of Swaziland.
Graeme:	There's encouraging news, the president is showing signs of recovery. There's a free phone number 0800 9494949494.
Craig:	The British Museum.
Heather:	This from Precious MacKenzie.
Amanda:	The President is conscious. He says "stop that weedy music, that's no help". He says there's only one kind of music that can help him now and I think you know what kind of music, it's not country, it's not western... let's rock!

[More random gifts arrive, are held up and the donor identified]

Heather:	George Best.
Craig:	Stevie Wonder.
Amanda:	Peter Mandleson.
Craig:	Jeff Koons.
Heather:	Steven Redgrave.
Amanda:	Julian Cope.

Heather: Nelson Mandela.
Craig: Roger Taylor with a message 'we will rock you'. You've heard Roger, get your party cards out! Let's rock him back. *[The audience each have a post card size programme, the reverse is silver and they are encouraged to wave theirs in the air]*

Jack Jones
[The President returns in an outrageously regal costume, to harp music, bubbles and a glitter ball. He sings a Jack Jones lounge classic]

President: I had a dream last night,
            What a lovely dream... *[etc.]*

[The President's cape is flown obscuring the stage.

Emperor's Validictory

President: Ecce Ergo Lux Regina In Magnificat. Sum Profundis key largo Id. Sprung Dieu Par Excelsus insignia, cum lars erotica benificant.
Plebian groundling fodder, sit fugal excalibal steelheart raison d'etre validiction for mort warrior ejaculata brevis, perpetual status quo in alter ego gluchlich. Supreme nova delinquant n'exeunt pa ad infinitum, hoc domini.
Gauche lies nothing, recht stands everything. Transubstantial sonic Cantor nations clang fire arbouritum.
Erectile fury sans exquisite nilhil vomitoria.
MC5 Jams makest le homme
In absentia meus cock et cererbllum flux ad infinitum
Volt face pa gloria, pa amore, pa maxima, pa treason angelica. Vita, vita, vita.

[Heather is brought back on and given a gun. The President persuades her to fire a shot at him. He catches the bullet in his teeth and brandishes it aloft.]

[The cape drops revealing the band in camp black militaristic uniforms. They play a punishingly direct number. The President dances, transported into an oblivious rictus ecstasy.]

President: Vita, vita, vita!

[Heather, having left the stage after firing the shot, has returned in uniform as part of the band.

The President dances off stage with Heather. Oblivious to the audience he dances with her following, through the auditorium and out into the night beyond]

[The band drive the final number on to its apocalyptic conclusion. They leave with the final mighty chord captured by the sound engineer so it echos and spirals around the empty stage before vanishing.

No curtain call.

No encore]

Lurid And Insane Credits

Party Members

<u>On Stage</u>
Violin : Amanda Hadingue
Bass : Graeme Rose
Keyboards : Craig Stephens
Voice : Andy Watson
Drums : Simon Webb
Guitar : Nina West

<u>Off Stage</u>
Testifying : Heather Burton
Original testimony : Sarah Dawson
Roadie plus : Emma Deegan
Uniforms : Helen Ingham
Lights plus : Paul Arvidson
Music direction : Brian Duffy
Direction : James Yarker with Amanda Hadingue
Photos : Ed Dimsdale
Print : Simon Ford
Education : Charlotte Goodwin

<u>Party Staff</u>
Emily Dawkes
Paulette Brian

People's Radio Freedom by Hamfisted!

<u>Party Thanks Due To:</u>
Blissbody
Nuffield Theatre Studio
Stan's Cafe board
Syd Ewart
Security Guards

Commissioned by Nuffield Theatre Studio

Comfort Hour

Comfort Hour was recorded as a lullaby for grown-ups who are scared of geopolitical instability, who can't sleep for professional anxiety or are haunted by personal insecurities. Like a poetic self-help tape *Comfort Hour* weaves a mantra of hollow reassurance through an evocative musical soundscape.

Comfort Hour was recorded live, directly onto mini-disc in late September 2001 by Stan's Cafe, a group of artists, musicians and actors, for their short term station, People's Radio Freedom. This hour long improvisation took place late at night in the company's rehearsal studio, looking out over the lights of Birmingham's industrial heartland, accompanied by the rumble of trains passing and the muffled sound of lorries in the distance.

Heather Burton - Voice
Amanda Hadingue - Violin
Graeme Rose - Bass
Craig Stephens - Keyboards
Andy Watson - Guitar
Simon Webb - Percussion
Nina West - Guitar

Text - James Yarker
Mix - Brian Duffy

Raw Text For Comfort Hour

This Is Comfort Hour.

Don't worry, everything will be fine.

No matter what anyone says,
whatever the papers say,
whatever the fear in the air,
everything will be all right.
This Is Comfort Hour.

There are no monsters under the bed,
there are no skeletons in the closet.
Any noise you hear is the friendly groaning of your shelter.
The rain won't touch you here.
The wind won't touch you here.
Snuggle up warm.
We are always here.
This voice is always be here.
I will always be here.

Listen.

The sun will always set and rise again.
The earth will always spin.
Clouds will always pass overhead.
The sea will always wash the shore.
Grass will always bend with the wind.
The stars will always stretch away.
The moon will always chart it's own course.
The sun will always set and rise again.
Some things change and other things will never change.

1, 2, 3, 4, 5, 6, 7, 8, 9, 10.

Everything will be alright.

James Yarker, September 2001

Performing Lurid and Insane

The halogens blazed. The 8 metre square steel door was hauled open by the 'bouncers' wearing t-shirts emblazoned with my Che Guevara style profile. My long hair blew in the wind, creating the impression that I'd just dismounted my helicopter.

This was it. The opening night of *Lurid and Insane* in a giant steel barn in the middle of nowhere. The heart was pounding. The mind was clear and bright. The smile was - ultra sincere. The band had been warming-up the crowd who'd been whipped into a near-frenzy by Amandas' cool and ecstatic stirrings. I entered the arena in the centre of a giant roving spotlight, ready to meet my first 'party member'. The idea was that the audience for the 'show' were the real audience for my (the Presidents) inauguration party. As I approached my first 'fan' to shake his hand, he - hugged me. Yes, he hugged me. Things couldn't have got off to a better start. It was probably one of the most challenging entrances of my life and this guy had just made it - perfect. I strode confidently and assuredly through the crowd, smiling and shaking hands, adrenaline fuelled by the crowd's reception and the loud rock-inspired fanfare being cannoned out by the band. This wasn't far from Elvis entering a Vegas arena to the strains of *Fanfare for the Common Man*.

Up on stage, I greeted the band one by one. The band were my 'cabinet' made up of sycophants who (as their 'testimonies' would later reveal) had nowhere else to go. On drums was Simon, the millionaire playboy who'd given me all his cash; on bass was Claude, the Austro/German traveller who'd hitched a ride in my Limo on the road to Mold; on violin was Amanda, the high flying business exec who'd been drinking herself towards oblivion until I'd 'saved' her; on green rock guitar was Nina, the dread headed maracas shaker, who (in order to get into the band and with no previous 'axe' experience) had learned how to play electrifying guitar riffs in only three days; on keyboards was Craig, the man who'd lived in a state of high anxiety, trepidation and fear until the day I'd turned him around (he also doubled as a roadie).

I stepped up to the mike, surveying the audience as I'd seen Mark E Smith do to a crowd of 2,000 at the London Forum on the night Germany beat England in 1996. I looked into the blackness. I looked into the light. I looked into - potential. The audience hung onto my every word as the ridiculously heightened opening speech describing my ascent to presidency flowed from my lips. And then, they moved in unison to the mighty opening anthem, chanting 'Welcome!'.

We hit the peak and changed gear instantly into the opening refrains of the fast and bluesy *Party Song*. The crowd jumped and grinned and jeered and leered-up at their new found idol for the night. Was this me? Was this Andy who'd gone into a kind of semi-retirement from performance? Was this Andy, who'd turned to Buddhism and found refuge in a life of renunciation and meditation? Was this Andy, who'd become quiet and restrained and preferred to draw circles in pencil than to get up on stage and energise? I sang my heart out and pushed the song to its limits.

We fired through the show, from the James Brown inspired *Work Love Groove* manifesto thang (a chance to re visit some of my disco-punk-rock-n-roll steps), through the band's testimonies (designed to get Heather our planted audience member up on stage to 'testify') into the fake hypnotism of the band, culminating in the ultra-sincere solo acoustic song ironically titled 'My Way', which climaxed into the President being 'shot' by an assassin in the audience and being dragged offstage.

The audience are led to believe that the President is fighting for his life. The band do everything they can to entice the crowd to help to "bring him back". They set-up a fake telethon type event, in which trash gifts are passed from the back of the space, through the audience and onto the stage. The gifts come from Elton John, Bill Gates, Madonna, Phil Collins and Brian May along with presents, e-mails and text messages from

Party members and international celebrities and politicians - including Nelson Mandela and Stephen & Pamela from Norwich.

Backstage, I remove the deep purple two tone satin suit and - quietly and carefully - put on each item of my pre-ceremonial outfit: the neatly pressed black military pants, the illuminated cummerbund, the scarlet military jacket festooned with LED's. I slick back my hair. And wait. How many times had I stood backstage waiting to go on? I try to stand still, intensely psyching myself up, silent and focused as the band members race around me, grabbing props and bumping into each other - a performance in itself, exposing the on/off stage instant persona flip. Beyond the curtain - noise, excitement and fluffy toys flow.

The crowd hits its frenzy-peak, demanding that the band 'BRING HIM BACK'. The atmosphere lulls. The lights dim, the crystal ball swirls and the President re-enters to croon the soft refrains of the strangely melancholic and surreal Jack Jones Vegas number *I Had a Dream*. The red LCDs flash on the military jacket. The gold-braid glistens. Smoke gathers. The audience and I are one.

The keyboard loops a soft loop, the trailing sparkling purple robe is fastened around my epauletted shoulders and raised to the height of the lighting grid, filling the full width and height of the stage. This creates a dazzlingly stylish backdrop to the Presidents' self-crowning ceremony (and conveniently hides the stage for a scene change). I give my inaugural speech - a chopped up mess of invented words and crown myself King with the biggest LCD encrusted crown you've ever seen. I'm so immersed in the moment, I forget what I'm supposed to do next, until my new wife (our 'planted' audience member Heather) joins me on stage. I offer her a loaded pistol and force her to shoot me as an act of devotion and faith. She is terrified, but obeys my command. I catch the bullet, smile manically at the audience and commence my journey into overdrive.

The band kicks-off, building a wall of sound like Sonic Youth embracing Slade. The new King spits out his self-invented manifesto as he breaks beyond megalomania into a shaking, gibbering tirade of memory cut-up and fantastic delusional edit. I'm suddenly aware that I'm going too far and might not come back. The Ian Curtis style static-bop becomes a psycho-physical embodiment of the Mark E Smith/ Henry Irving venom/ expulsion and - I'm ok. The King takes the hand of His Queen, struts the Mick Jagger stage-strut down into His crowd - and exits. With a mighty bow!

PS - He was last seen by the crew wandering through the blackness t'ord a freezing shed-cum-dressing room by a boggy marsh.

Andy Watson, October 2005

Marginal Notes

Performance for ArtsFest, Birmingham, August 1999

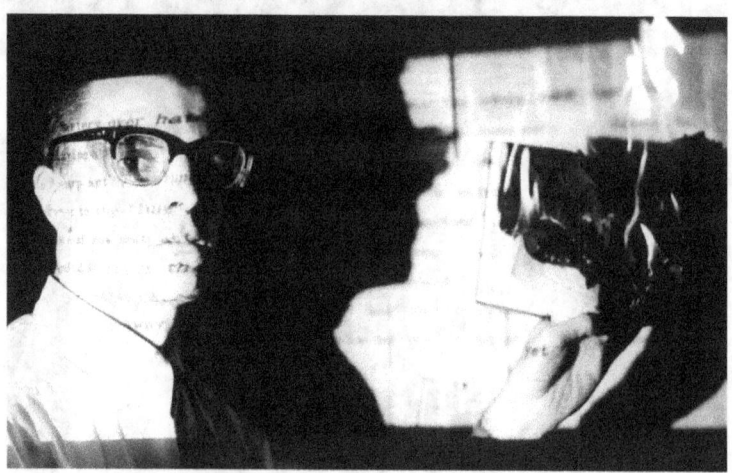

"And further more their influence is beginning to spread. Evidence of their work is growing; soon it will be everywhere we look. They are teaching our children, publishing their manifestos and no one is watching, no one is protecting us from the dissemination of their ideas. They didn't come from here and they don't belong here - they take and they give nothing back. They might live in your street, be your neighbours or be sat next to you in this fine building. Perhaps one of them is talking to you now. You can hear them through the walls of your home, see them driving around the city, playing football in the park, sat talking at the next table in the pub. They may look at you and smile. Do not meet their gaze, they can see right through you. Do not speak to them, they will steal your voice.

They will invite you to go along with them, to meet them halfway, cross the threshold, leap into the unknown. They claim to offer an alternative vision but it's dangerous mumbo-jumbo. They are chancers, they play on our naïveté. If you laugh you are lying to yourself. Their search for receptive minds in which to propagate their ideas is ceaseless and the number of their followers is multiplying. They nurture them carefully to allow them to thrive, prosper and proliferate. You may not believe this, you may say, "I know my mind. I know myself. I would not do these things. I would not think these thoughts. These things are beyond me" and yet, and yet, we are all capable - if you are capable of thought you are capable of action. You may say to yourself "I will try it. It's only an hour out of my life" but what an hour and what things can happen in an hour? You may feel curious, teased, you may feel compassion, you may even allow yourselves to believe them; do not. Do not indulge them. "I know their type" you might say "I know them" but to know is one thing, to engage another still. Do not be seduced by them. Do not let them touch you.

Do you lack something in your lives? Sir - do you feel a lack? Madam, do you feel a void at the heart of your life? Aside from material wealth, from our religious faith, from our personal relationships, aside from these things, do we feel a lack, a gap that needs filling? I believe we do not. We are complete and yet they encourage us to want more, to depend on more - and what more is that? It is that, of course, which only they can supply.

I stand here and I ask you to listen to me and to believe me. Occasionally I revert to metaphor and you might say I am acting. There the confusion starts.

And now, Mr Stephens, you ask, what can we do to rid this great land of ours of this malignant race? Starve them. Starve them of money, of faith, of social contact. Hound them out of your circle, point to them in your streets, brand them 'actor', 'artist', 'deceiver', 'hypocrite'. Do not let them spread. Their growth will be pernicious. Shut down the theatres. If you can ever find it, shut down Stan's Cafe.

Thank you."

Performed by Craig Stephen and written by James Yarker

Come Together

Unlimited set a number of companies the challenge of creating a piece of theatre in response to a favourite musical track of their choosing. The implication was that each piece would be performed to the track and, unable to imagine a satisfying relationship between the music and theatre in this way, we politely declined the invitation.

Unlimited's challenge continued to niggle at me. Speculating as to what track we would have chosen my thoughts kept returning to Primal Scream's *Come Together* as featured on their seminal album, *Screamadelica*. This ten minute long track is essentially an anthemic groove with a gospel refrain and heavy sampling of a speech given by the Reverend Jesse Jackson.

A bit of research tracked the samples to a recording of Jackson opening of Wattstax, a festival of Black music staged at the Los Angeles Coliseum in 1972. A trawl of YouTube allowed us to watch the original speech. In its full form the speech is a powerful invocation of black pride but in its sampling the racial politics has been edited out, leaving it as a simple feel good celebration of music's power to bring people together (hence, presumably, the track's title). Shocked and fired up by this 'rewriting' we approached Unlimited and humbly asked if we could accept their commission after all.

The Stan's Cafe version of *Come Together* withdraws the music from the audience, instead Graeme Rose, as politician or preacher or even record executive, delivers Rev. Jackson's text live, as it appears on the Primal Scream track, mostly from behind a table but ultimately standing at the front edge of the stage. Lucy Nicholls delivers the female vocal line "All together, as one", again synchronising with the unheard track, but speaking not singing the lines. Lucy appears to be an acolyte of Graeme's, sat behind and to his right. Craig Stephens, possibly a bodyguard, sat behind Graeme but to his left, embodies the rest of the track. He taps the high hat pattern out on his knee and other musical lines are translated into physical equivalents.

At the close of the piece, when the performance of the track is finished, the Rev. Jackson is heard over the P.A. Delivering a section of his speech not used on the record which speaks about black people and black power, making clear the racial context of the original material.

Come Together was performed at Pilot Night, an evening of 'scratch' performances. There was nothing 'scratch' about ours but where else can you perform a 10 minutes long show? The audience was a mixed crowd, fans of musicals and comedies. *Come Together* stood out in that context, very tense, highly charged, restrained, quite still and for long periods, silent. Craig wore an ear piece through which he listened to the original track played very quietly, allowing him to keep time. Graeme and Lucy repeating the same lines over and over forced new and changing meanings from the words, as challenging live as they are blissfully comforting on record.

The whiteness of our performers mirrors Primal Scream's whiteness. Our appropriation of their appropriation concludes with our giving the text back to its black originator. The victory of Barack Obama in the US presidential election one month earlier was fresh in our minds and gave the show an extra spin.

Times	Rev. Jesse Jackson	Choir	Percussion
4"	This is a beautiful day		
	It is a new day		
16"	We are together		
23"	We are unified and of one accord		
34"	Because together we got power apart we got pow wow		
45"	Today on this program you will hear Gospel and Rhythm and Blues and Jazz		
	All those are just labels we know that music is music		Siren
1'24"			End Siren
1'54"			Siren
2' 16"	Today on this program you will hear Gospel and Rhythm and Blues and Jazz		
	All those are just labels we know that music is music.		End Siren
2'34"	Gospel, Gospel, Gospel, Gospel, Gospel.		Siren End Siren
3'18"			Blares Start
3'49"	(Whisper) Gospel, gospel and Soul (?)		
4'31"			Drop All
4'48"		All Together As One	
4'58"		All Together As One	
		All Together As One	Brass
		All Together As One	
		All Together As One	Brass
		All Together As One	Brass
5' 42"	This is a beautiful day it is a new day	All Together As One	Brass
	This is a beatiful day it is a new day	All Together As One	Brass
	We are together, we are together, we are unified, we are together	All Together As One	
		All Together As One	
6' 10"	Because together we have power apart we've got power	All Together As One	
	We are together	All Together As One	

6'28"	Today on this programme you will hear gospal and rhythm and blues and jazz	All Together As One
	All those are just labels we know that music is music	All Together As One
6'51"	Gospel, Gospel, Gospel, Gospel.	All Together As One
		All Together As One Brass
	We are together, we are unified, we are together	All Together As One
		All Together As One
		All Together As One
		All Together As One
		All Together As One
		All Together As One
8'16"	The name of the game is power,	All Together As One
	If you ain't playing power you're in the wrong place	
	Brothers and sisters, the name of the game is power	All Together As One
	If you ain't playing power you're in the wrong place	
	Brothers and sisters, the name of the game is power	All Together As One
	If you ain't playing power you're in the wrong place	
	Brothers and sisters, the name of the game is power	All Together As One
	If you ain't playing power you're in the wrong place	
	Brothers and sisters, the name of the game is power	All Together As One
	If you ain't playing power you're in the wrong place	
	We are together	All Together As One
	We are together, we are unified, we are together	All Together As One
	Gospel, Gospel, Gospel, We are together	All Together As One
		All Together As One Brass
		All Together As One Brass
		All Together As One
		All Together As One

About the illustration and design

The illustrations for the covers of these books were undertaken by students at Birmingham City University as the final module of their first-year illustration course during the Spring/Summer of 2018. The images were developed using workshops using variations of the theatre-devising methods produced by Stan's Cafe but adapted and applied to the making of visual work. The resulting work was shown in the pop-up exhibition *The Something Of Somebody Something* at AE Harris in May 2018.

The design concept of the books was produced by final year Graphic Design student Aimee Chapman. These were then further developed for print in a collaborative process between Stan's Cafe and the University's Innovation Product Support Service (IPSS) and involved helping the company with selecting appropriate DTP software, undertaking training and selecting a suitable print on demand service.

Gareth Courage
Lecturer in Illustration
Birmingham City University

www.ingramcontent.com/pod-product-compliance
Lightning Source LLC
Chambersburg PA
CBHW071758080526
44588CB00013B/2292